316385

D0591301

Introducing Religions

Judaism

Sue Penney

www.heinemann.co.uk/library
Visit our website to find out more information about Heinemann Library books.

To order:
☎ Phone 44 (0) 1865 888066
📄 Send a fax to 44 (0) 1865 314091
💻 Visit the Heinemann Bookshop at www.heinemann.co.uk/library to browse our catalogue and order online.

First published in Great Britain by Heinemann Library, Halley Court, Jordan Hill, Oxford OX2 8EJ, part of Harcourt Education.
Heinemann is a registered trademark of Harcourt Education Ltd.

© Sue Penney, 2006
The moral right of the proprietor has been asserted.

All rights reserved. No part of this publication may be reproduced, stored in a retrieval system, or transmitted in any form or by any means, electronic, mechanical, photocopying, recording, or otherwise, without either the prior written permission of the publishers or a licence permitting restricted copying in the United Kingdom issued by the Copyright Licensing Agency Ltd, 90 Tottenham Court Road, London W1T 4LP (www.cla.co.uk).

Editorial: Clare Lewis
Design: Jo Hinton-Malivoire and Q2A Creative
Illustrations: Gecko Limited
Picture Research: Erica Newbury
Production: Helen McCreath

Printed and bound in China by WKT.

10 digit ISBN 0 431 06654 X
13 digit ISBN 978 0 431 06654 7
10 09 08 07 06
10 9 8 7 6 5 4 3 2 1

British Library Cataloguing in Publication Data
Penney, Sue
Judaism (Introducing Religions – 2nd edition)
296
A full catalogue record for this book is available from the British Library.

Acknowledgements
The publishers would like to thank the following for permission to reproduce photographs:
The Ancient Art and Architecture Collection p. 43; Werner Braun pp. 44 (top), 46 (top), 48; J Allan Cash Photo Library p. 36; Circa Photo Library pp. 16, 21; Bruce Coleman Ltd p. 29; Corbis p. 23; A H Edwards/Circa Photo Library p. 17; Getty Images p. 22; Robert Harding pp. 10, 42; Robert Harding/E Simanor p. 12; The Hutchison Library p. 20; The Jewish Museum p. 27; B Key/Christine Osborne Pictures p. 41; Peter Osborne p. 44 (below); Zev Radovan pp. 37, 38; Anat Rotem-Braun p. 24; Barrie Searle/Circa Photo Library pp. 15, 31, 33, 35; Juliette Soester pp. 14, 32, 46 (below), 49, 51; The Weiner Library p. 40; Zefa pp. 11, 13, 15, 22 (top), 24, 26, 30, 50.

The photograph on the previous page is reproduced by permission of Corbis/Royalty Free Images.

Cover photograph of Orthodox Jewish boys studying the Torah in Jerusalem, reproduced with permission of Getty Images/Tom Stoddart.

The publishers would like to thank Gillian Fisher for her assistance in the preparation of this book.

Every effort has been made to contact copyright holders of any material reproduced in this book. Any omissions will be rectified in subsequent printings if notice is given to the publishers.

The paper used to print this book comes from sustainable resources.

Contents

Words that are printed in bold, **like this**, are explained in the glossary on page 50.

MAP: where the main religions began

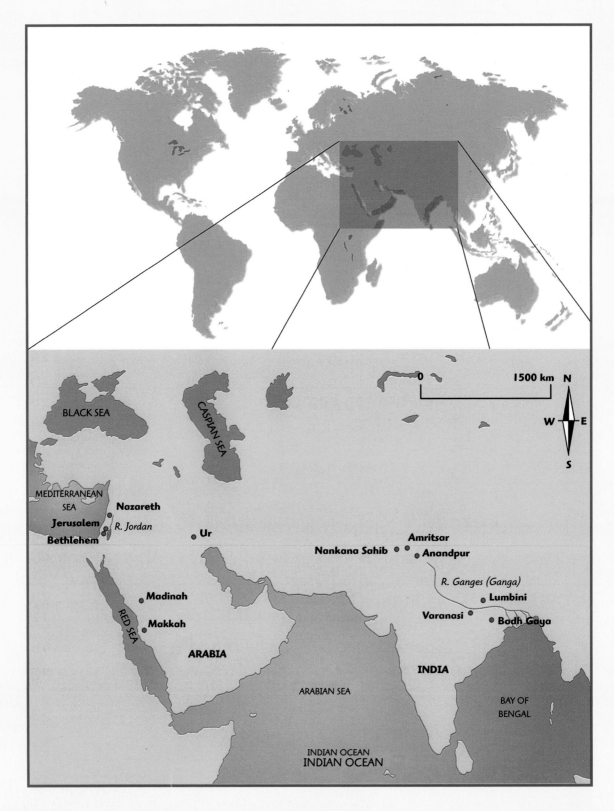

BLACK SEA

CASPIAN SEA

MEDITERRANEAN SEA

Nazareth

Jerusalem

R. Jordan

Bethlehem

Ur

Amritsar

Nankana Sahib

Anandpur

R. Ganges (Ganga)

Lumbini

Madinah

Varanasi

Bodh Gaya

RED SEA

Makkah

ARABIA

INDIA

ARABIAN SEA

BAY OF BENGAL

INDIAN OCEAN
INDIAN OCEAN

0   1500 km

N
W · E
S

TIMECHART: when the main religions began

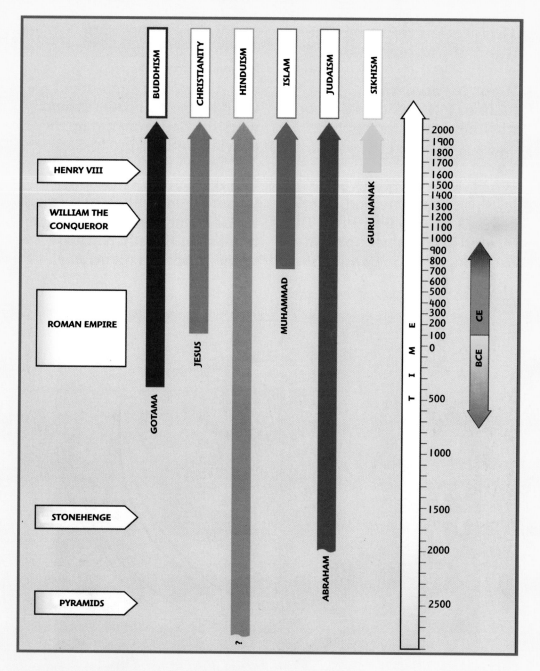

Note about dating systems *In this book dates are not called* BC *and* AD, *which is the Christian dating system. The letters* BCE *and* CE *are used instead.* BCE *stands for "Before the Common Era" and* CE *stands for "Common Era".* BCE *and* CE *can be used by people of all religions, Christians too. The year numbers are not changed.*

Introducing Judaism

This section tells you something about Jewish belief.

What is Judaism?

Judaism is the religion of people who are Jews. It is one of the oldest religions in the world.

What do Jews believe?

Jews believe in one God. They believe that God is a **spirit**. That means God does not have a body like a person or animal does.

God was never born and will never die. He sees and knows everything. God made everything, and cares about what he made. People should **worship** God. Worship means praying and talking to God.

What do Jews call God?

Jews have more than one name for God, but they use one name more than the others. This name is **Adonai** ("Lord").

It shows how much Jews respect God. Jews believe that God's name is important. They never use it carelessly.

A modern sculpture of a menorah

The Shema

The **Shema** is the prayer Jews use most often. It reminds Jews how much they must love God. Jews believe that God gave them rules which they must obey so that God will look after them.

Signs which Jews use

There are two signs which Jews often use. One is a special candlestick with seven arms, which is called a **menorah**. The other is a star which has six points. It is sometimes called the Star of David.

The Star of David

The Shema

The Shema is the prayer which Jews use most. Jews use it in their own prayers at home in the morning, and in the last prayers they say before they go to sleep at night. It is used in the morning and evening services in the synagogue, too. It is made up of three sections of the **Torah** (see pages 14–15). The Shema reminds Jews how important it is to love God.

The Shema is quite long, but it begins like this:

Hear, Israel, the Lord is our God. The Lord is one. Now you must love the Lord your God with all your heart and with all your soul and with all your strength.

(Deuteronomy chapter 6 verses 4–5)

The synagogue

This section tells you about the place where Jews meet to worship God.

A **synagogue** is the place where Jews meet to **worship** God. It is also used as a school to teach children about the Jewish religion and as a meeting place for concerts, clubs, and other social activities.

The Holy Ark

The most important thing in a synagogue is the **Holy Ark**. This is a special cupboard at the front of the main hall. The **scrolls** are kept in the Ark.

Scrolls

A scroll is like a book with one long page. The writing on it is carefully done by hand. To read the writing, you unroll the page. Each end of the scroll is wound onto a wooden roller.

Scrolls are very precious. The **Torah** is written on them. Another name for the Torah is the Books of Teaching. They are the most important Jewish holy books. The scrolls are taken out of the Ark when people meet for worship, and carried from the Ark to the **bimah**. When they are put away in the Ark, they are wrapped in beautiful covers.

Inside a modern orthodox synagogue. (The upstairs is the women's part.)

The Ark is at the front of the synagogue.

The lamp

In front of the Ark is a special lamp, called Ner Tamid. It is never allowed to go out. This reminds Jews that God is always there with them.

The bimah

The bimah is a raised part of the floor in front of the Ark. It has a reading desk where the Torah is placed to be read.

The women's part

In most synagogues, women sit in a separate part of their own.

Scrolls

A scroll is made from a long piece of parchment. This is animal skin that is dried and smoothed out so it can be written on. The ends are sewn round wooden rollers. Each scroll is about 60 metres (200 feet) from one end to the other. The person reading the scroll uses a special pointer so they can follow the words without touching the parchment with their hands.

When the scrolls are put away in the Holy Ark, they are covered with special cloths called mantles. Mantles are made of silk or velvet and are covered with beautiful embroidery. The ends of the wooden rollers are decorated, too. They have bells and crowns on them. This is all to show how important the scrolls are.

Worship in the synagogue

This section tells you about how Jews worship in the synagogue.

Jews believe that **worshipping** God is very important. They pray to God, and ask for help or give thanks for the things he has done for them. Jews believe they can worship anywhere, but the **synagogue** is a special place.

Many Jews go to the synagogue on a Friday evening and Saturday morning. The Jewish **holy** day begins on a Friday evening and lasts until Saturday evening.

Synagogue service
A **service** is a special meeting for worship. A synagogue service has readings from the holy books, prayers, and **psalms**.

At some services, there are readings from the **Torah**.

This man is wearing tefillin for worship.

Tefillin

Tefillin are the small black leather boxes which are worn at morning prayers by some Jewish men. Inside the boxes are tiny **scrolls** which contain four parts of writings from the Torah. Each box has a very long strap, which is used to tie it on. One tefillah (tefillin is more than one tefillah) is tied to the top of the left arm so it points at the heart.

The other one is tied to the forehead, just above where the hair begins. Wearing tefillin reminds Jews that they should love God with all their heart and with all their mind. It reminds them how important their feelings and their thoughts are. Tefillin are always handled with great care and respect. They are checked regularly to make sure the scrolls are in good condition.

A tefillah with its contents.

Special clothes

At services in the synagogue, men wear a cap called a **kippah**. It shows respect for God. At morning services, men wear a **tallit**, too. This is a prayer shawl, rather like a large scarf. It is sometimes called a prayer robe. It is usually made of silk or wool, with fringes at each end.

In some synagogues, men wear two small black leather boxes, called **tefillin**. They wear one on the middle of their forehead. The other is fastened to their arm, facing their heart.

Jewish holy books

This section tells you about the holy books.

The most important books for a religion are often called the **holy** books. Holy means respected because it is to do with God.

The Jewish holy books are divided into three parts. The first part is the Books of Teaching, called the **Torah**. The second part is the Books of the **Prophets**. The third part is the Books of **Writings**.

The Torah

The books of the Torah are the most important books for Jews. They are the ones written on **scrolls** for reading in the **synagogue**. There are stories about how the world was made, and about the **Patriarchs**, the very first Jews.

There are also rules which teach Jews how they should live. This is why the books are called Torah, which means the Books of Teaching.

Altogether there are 613 rules. Many Jews try to keep them all.

Scrolls with their mantles and decorations

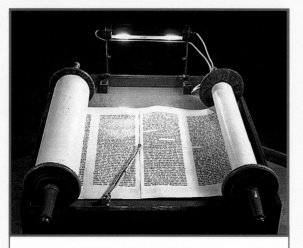

A scroll on the **bimah**. The pointer is used when reading it.

The Books of the Prophets

Jews believe that the **prophets** were men and women who were given special powers by God. Jews believe that what the prophets said is still important for people today.

The Books of Writings

These books contain stories from Jewish history. The best known of these books is the Book of **Psalms**. Psalms are often used in worship in the synagogue.

Jewish writing

The holy books of the Jews are written in **Hebrew**. Hebrew is written starting at the right hand side of the page and going to the left. So, reading a Hebrew book is like reading from the back to the front.

Below you can see some words written in Hebrew, and what they mean.

תורה	Torah
מגילה	scroll
כפה	kippah
טלית	tallit
חלה	challah bread
בית-כנסת	synagogue
שבת	Shabbat
שופר	shofar
מזוזה	mezuzah

There are 23 letters in the Hebrew alphabet, but when reading Hebrew, you need to take great care. Some letters change their sound if a dot is placed on top, under or next to them. For example, בּ is said like a B, but ב is said like a V.

Shabbat

This section tells you about the Jewish day of worship.

Shabbat is the Jewish day of rest and **worship**. It begins when the sun sets on a Friday evening, and lasts until sunset on Saturday.

Why do Jews celebrate Shabbat?
Jews believe that God made the world in six days. On the seventh day, God rested. Saturday is the seventh day, so Jews remember God by resting on this day, too.

How do Jews celebrate Shabbat?
On Fridays, Jews clean the house and prepare for the special Shabbat meal.

At sunset, the wife or mother of the family lights two candles, and says a prayer. Shabbat has begun! Many Jews go to the **synagogue**, then come home to eat the special meal together. Before the meal, the husband or father of the family says prayers.

The Shabbat meal is the most important part of the week for Jews. The table has a clean white cloth, and the food is the best the family can afford. There are always two loaves of special bread. This is called **challah bread**. Families may spend all evening eating and chatting. It is a very happy time.

Lighting the Shabbat candles. Notice the challah bread under its cover.

The havdalah ceremony, with candle and spice box

The day of rest

The **Torah** tells Jews that they should rest on Shabbat. Many Jews follow this rule very carefully. Resting means more than just not working. They do not drive, or go shopping. All food is prepared the day before, because cooking is not allowed. Some Jews will not switch on a light or use the telephone except in an emergency.

This makes Shabbat special. Jews can spend the day with family or friends without feeling that there are things they must do. Shabbat ends on a Saturday evening, when the father says more prayers.

Special prayers for Shabbat

The prayer that the father says as the meal begins is called the kiddush. The kiddush praises God, and thanks God that Jews can share in Shabbat. The prayers that are said at the end of Shabbat are called the **havdalah**. Before the father says the havdalah, the family lights a special plaited candle.

Everyone sniffs a special box of spices, too. They smell very pleasant, and the smell spreads all through the house. This is a way of showing that Jews hope the peace and quiet of Shabbat will last all through the coming week. After the havdalah prayer, the candle is put out by dipping it in a cup of wine.

Rosh Hashanah

This section tells you about the most important days of the Jewish year.

Rosh Hashanah
Rosh Hashanah is the Jewish New Year. Jews have their own calendar, so Jewish New Year is in September or early October. The night before Rosh Hashanah, Jews have a special meal at home. As well as ordinary food, they eat apples dipped in honey. This is a way of saying that everyone hopes the year that is beginning will be sweet. There is also a special service in the **synagogue**.

The **shofar** is blown. A shofar is made from a ram's horn. It sounds solemn, a bit like a trumpet. It reminds people that God is important.

The High Holy Days
Rosh Hashanah is the beginning of the most serious time of year for Jews. It is the beginning of 10 special days called the High Holy Days. They are days when Jews think about the things they have done wrong in the past year. They make promises to themselves and to God that they will do better in future.

Apples and honey for Rosh Hashanah

The shofar

The shofar is a special musical instrument which is used in the synagogue at Rosh Hashanah and Yom Kippur. It is made from a ram's horn. More than one shofar are called shofarot.

Shofarot come in different sizes – an average one is about 32 cm (12.5 inches) long. There are strict rules about how to make a shofar. The horn is warmed, then hollowed out. The end is cut off to make a hole that the person can blow through. A shofar sounds a bit like a trumpet or a hunting horn with a low note. It is very loud and solemn.

One reason why shofarot are important to Jews is because they have been used for thousands of years – almost from the beginning of Judaism.

Blowing the shofar

Yom Kippur

The 10th High Holy Day is called Yom Kippur. This is the day when Jews ask God to forgive them for all the things they have done wrong.

They often spend a lot of the day in the synagogue, and they **fast** for the whole day. This means they do not eat or drink anything. It is a way of showing how sorry they are. Jews believe that God will forgive them if they are really sorry, so at Yom Kippur they also remember how much God loves them.

Sukkot

This section tells you about the festival of Sukkot.

A **sukkah** is a sort of three-sided hut. (Sukkot is the word for more than one sukkah.) A sukkah is usually made of wood. The most important part is the roof. It is covered in leaves or branches, but must be open enough so you can see the sky. For the festival of Sukkot, Jews build a sukkah in their garden or at the **synagogue**. They live in it for the week of the festival.

A sukkah

Why do Jews build sukkot?

Thousands of years ago, Jews had no fixed home. They spent many years living in a desert. Some Jews probably had tents. Many others had to build somewhere to live themselves. They built sukkot. Today, Jews build sukkot to remind themselves of when Jews long ago had nowhere else to live.

Carrying the lulav and citron

The lulav

There is a special synagogue **service** at Sukkot. Everyone holds branches of three trees in their left hand, and they carry a citron in their right hand. Citrons are similar to lemons. During the service, people walk around the synagogue carrying the citron and waving the branches. The branches and the citron stand for parts of the body. Joining them together reminds Jews that they must **worship** God with all their body.

Simchat Torah

Simchat **Torah** is the day after the end of Sukkot. It is a day when Jews think especially about the Torah. Part of the Torah is read every week in the synagogue. Simchat Torah is the day when the last part of the Torah is read, and the readings start from the beginning again. It is a happy day when children are given sweets and fruit.

The lulav

The lulav is the collection of branches that people hold at the synagogue service for Sukkot. The branches are from the palm, the willow, and the myrtle.

Each branch has a meaning. The palm tree stands for the spine, the backbone. The willow stands for the lips. The myrtle stands for the eyes. The branches are held in one hand, and the citron is held in the other. The citron stands for the heart. Together, they remind Jews that they must worship God with all their body.

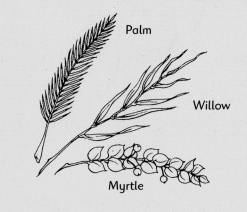

Palm

Willow

Myrtle

Hanukkah

This section tells you about the festival of Hanukkah.

The festival of **Hanukkah** lasts for eight days. It almost always takes place at the beginning of December, though the dates change from year to year. It is celebrated with special games, presents, and parties.

The story of Hanukkah

Hanukkah reminds Jews of things which happened many hundreds of years ago.

In those days, the Jews' country had been taken over. The new king was wicked and cruel. The worst thing was, he did not allow Jews to **worship** God. He said they had to worship him instead.

A group of Jews fought against the king, led by a man called Judah. Judah's tiny army managed to beat the king's soldiers in a battle. Now the Jews had control of the city of Jerusalem. This was important because it was where the **Temple** was. The Temple was the most important place in the Jewish religion. The king had spoiled the Temple so that God could not be worshipped there.

Judah wanted to make the Temple right again. It had to be carefully cleaned before the menorah could be lit. This was the Temple lamp, which had seven branches. It was supposed to burn all the time, but the king had let it go out. When the soldiers came to light it again, they found that there was only enough oil in it for one night. The oil was special, and it took eight days to get some more.

Lighting the candles at Hanukkah

A Hanukiah and dreidles

But the lamp stayed alight all the time! The people said that God made it burn because he was so pleased to be worshipped in the Temple again.

Celebrating Hanukkah

Jews use a special candlestick to celebrate Hanukkah. It is called a **hanukiah**. It holds eight candles and an extra one which is used to light all the others. On the first night of the festival, they light one candle, on the second night two, and so on, until the last night of the festival, when all nine are lit. As they light the candles, they say special prayers.

The dreidle game

The dreidle is a sort of spinning top which Jewish children play with at Hanukkah. It has four sides. On each side, there is a letter from the Jewish alphabet. When all the letters are put together, they make the first letters of the words which say "A great miracle happened there", meaning in Israel.

To play the dreidle game, children have a pile of sweets and spin the dreidle. The letter it lands on tells them whether to take all the sweets, half of them, give back what they have, or do nothing.

Purim

This section tells you about the festival of Purim.

Purim takes place in February or March. The story told at Purim happened hundreds of years ago. A man called Haman lived in a country called Persia, now called Iran. He helped the king to rule the country. Haman knew he was very important and made the most of it. He wanted everybody to bow when he passed! Some Jews were living in Persia then.

Jews believe that bowing means **worship**, and it is wrong to worship anyone but God. One day, Haman saw a Jew who did not bow to him. Haman was very angry and wanted to punish him. He decided to ask the king to order that all Jews in Persia should be killed! The king agreed.

The king's wife, who was called Esther, heard about this. She was Jewish, but the king did not know that.

A play for Purim

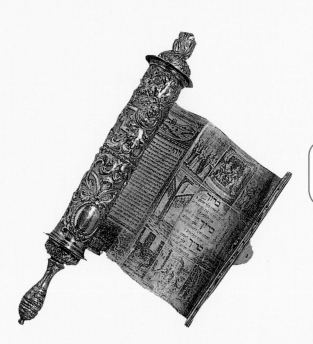

This scroll of the Book of Esther is in the Jewish Museum in London.

She knew she had to get the king to change his mind. Esther asked the king and Haman to come to a special meal. She told the king the real reason why Haman wanted to kill the Jews. The king was very angry. He ordered that Haman be killed instead. All the Jews were saved.

Celebrating Purim

At Purim, the story of Haman and Esther is read in the **synagogue**. Every time children hear the name of Haman, they make as much noise as they can. They shout, whistle, and stamp their feet. They use special rattles called **greggors**. The idea is to make so much noise that no one can hear the name Haman. Children often take part in plays or go to fancy dress parties.

Purim customs

Purim is a time for sharing, and at Purim Jews often give money to people who are very poor. As well as giving money, everyone sends gifts of food to their family and friends. This means that everyone can share in the festival.

One of the special foods eaten at Purim is a sweet called Hamantaschen, which means "Haman's purses". They are made of pastry with a sweet filling, and are shaped like the purses that people used to have long ago.

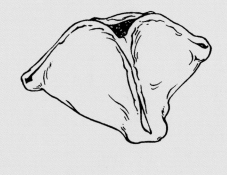

Pesach

This section tells you about the story of Pesach, the festival of Passover.

Pesach is the most important Jewish festival. The story that Jews remember at Pesach happened over 3,500 years ago. Jews then were living in the country called Egypt. The king of Egypt made the Jews work for him. They had to work very hard, and he did not pay them. They were beaten with whips.

One of the Jews was a man called Moses. He believed that God wanted him to go and tell the king to let the Jews go. Moses went to the king, and told him that he must free the Jews. The king did not like the Jews, but he wanted to keep his workers. He refused.

The plagues

After this, awful things started to happen in Egypt. When things go wrong like this, it is called a **plague.**

The 10 plagues

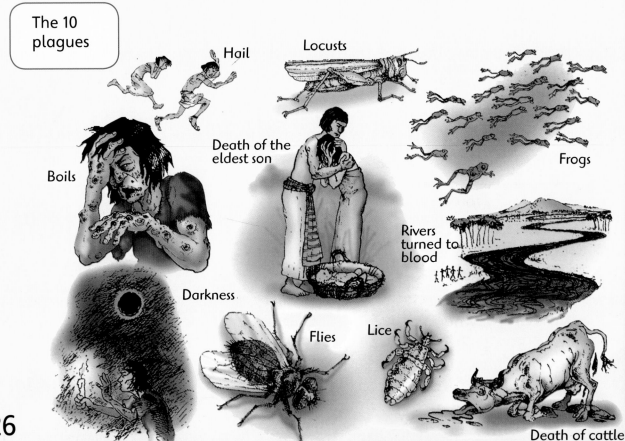

Hail

Locusts

Boils

Death of the eldest son

Frogs

Rivers turned to blood

Darkness

Flies

Lice

Death of cattle

There were 10 plagues. Everyone believed these had been sent by God. Each time there was a plague, the king said the Jews could go. But when the plague stopped, he changed his mind.

In the last plague, the eldest boy in every Egyptian family died. The king said the Jews really could go. They left, but then the king sent his army after them. The Jews were saved because the water in the Sea of Reeds parted for them. When the water flooded back, the Egyptian soldiers drowned.

One of the plagues was a swarm of locusts.

The 10 plagues

While Moses was trying to persuade the king to let the Jews go, there were 10 plagues in Egypt. Before each plague, Moses warned the king what was going to happen.

The first plague was that all the rivers and water turned to blood. The second plague was frogs everywhere. The third plague was lice. The fourth plague was flies. The fifth plague was when all the farm animals died. The sixth plague was when all the people became covered with enormous painful spots. The seventh plague was hailstorms. The eighth plague was locusts. Locusts are small flying insects which eat leaves and crops. Then there was a plague of darkness, when the sun did not shine. The last plague was the death of the eldest son in every Egyptian family, including the king's.

Celebrating Pesach

This section tells you about how Jews celebrate Pesach or Passover.

The most important part of the celebrations is a meal. This is called the **Seder**. It is a normal meal, but it always includes many things which are special.

The four questions

As the family eat the meal, they tell the story of the first Pesach. The youngest child in the family always asks four questions. The first question is "Why is this night different from all other nights?" The other questions are about the foods they are eating and why they are special. These questions are answered as the family tells the story.

Special things on the table

One of the most important things on the table is the Seder plate. It has five parts. It holds five things which remind Jews of things that happened to the Jews in Egypt.

There is a dish which holds **matzot**. Matzot are "cakes" of bread that has been made without any **leaven**. Leaven is the ingredient that makes bread rise. Matzot are flat and quite crisp, like crackers. Jews do not eat anything that contains leaven during Pesach.

The Seder meal

The Seder plate with matzot

There is also a bowl of salty water. Salt water is like tears. This is not to drink, it is to remind Jews how unhappy the Jews in Egypt were. Each person has a glass for wine. They drink wine four times while they are eating the meal, because God promised four times to bring them out of Egypt.

A family occasion

The Seder is a serious meal, because it reminds Jews of their history. But it is also a time when families can enjoy being together. When they have finished eating, families often stay at the table and sing songs. The songs have repeated words or choruses, so even tiny children can enjoy joining in. During the meal, a piece of matzah is hidden in the room. At the end of the meal, the children hunt for the piece and the finder gets a prize. The songs and games all help to make Pesach a special time.

The Seder plate

The first thing on the Seder plate is a lamb bone. It is not eaten, but it reminds Jews of the lambs killed in Egypt. A hard-boiled egg roasted in a flame reminds Jews of animals which were once killed as an offering to God. A green vegetable, usually parsley or lettuce, reminds them of the way God cared for the Jews in the desert. Bitter herbs, usually horseradish, are a reminder of how unhappy the Jews were in Egypt.

The fifth thing is charoset, a sweet mixture of apples, nuts, and wine. It is a paste, so it reminds Jews of the mortar which Jews used when they were building for the king. It is also sweet, so it reminds Jews of the happiness of escaping from Egypt.

Shavuot

This section tells you about the festival of Shavuot.

This synagogue has been decorated for Shavuot.

The festival of Shavuot is held seven weeks after Pesach. This is why it is sometimes called the **Feast of Weeks**. At Shavuot, Jews remember a story from the **Torah**. The story is about how God gave Moses 10 rules that tell people how they should live.

An important rule is called a **commandment**, so these special rules are called the **Ten Commandments**. Jews believe that the Ten Commandments are very important.

Ladder bread, which is special for Shavuot

The Ten Commandments

The Ten Commandments are long, but they can be summed up like this.

1 I am the Lord your God. You must not have any gods but me.
2 You must not make any idols (statues) to worship.
3 You must not use God's name carelessly.
4 Remember to keep **Shabbat** as a special day.
5 Respect your father and mother.
6 You must not kill.
7 You must not have affairs.
8 You must not steal.
9 You must not tell lies about other people.
10 You must not be jealous of what other people have.

In the synagogue

At Shavuot, **synagogues** are always beautifully decorated with flowers and fruit.

There is a special **service** when the story is read from the Torah about how Moses went up a mountain to talk to God. When Moses came back to the other Jews, God had given him the Ten Commandments.

At home

After this service in the synagogue, Jews go home for a special meal.

Like other festival meals, there is always bread which has been baked for that meal. The bread baked for Shavuot has a ladder shape on it. This is to remind people that Moses had to climb the mountain to talk to God.

31

Early Jewish history

This section tells you a little about the early history of the Jews.

Jewish history began thousands of years ago. No one person ever "began" the religion we call Judaism. People had ideas which grew little by little. The ideas became beliefs. The people became sure that what they believed came from God. They began to live in a way which showed what they believed. Beliefs were passed down from parents to children. Over hundreds of years, these beliefs came to be called the Jewish faith.

Early leaders

The two most important men in the early history of the Jews were Abraham and Moses. You can find out more about Abraham on pages 34–35, and there is more about Moses on pages 36–37.

Kings

After they had escaped from Egypt, the Jews lived in the desert for many years. At last, they made their home in a country called Canaan. This was in the area that today we call Israel. For hundreds of years, they were ruled by kings. Some kings were very good rulers. Others were not.

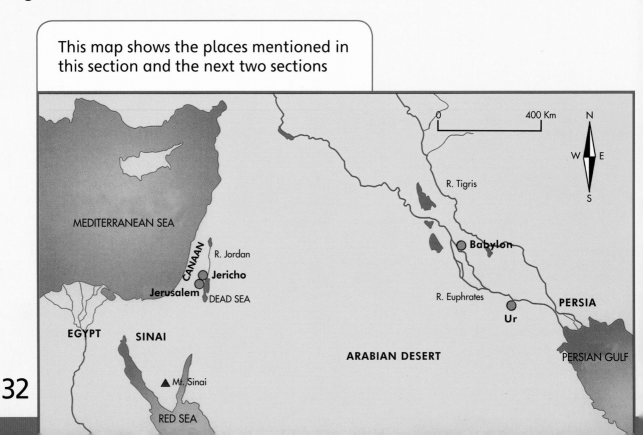

This map shows the places mentioned in this section and the next two sections

Jews today come from all parts of the world. This boy comes from Ethiopia.

One of the kings was called David. He made the country rich and powerful.

Many Jews still believe that David was the best king the Jews have ever had.

Prophets

As well as the kings, there were other men and women who are important in Jewish history. They are the **prophets**. The prophets told people what God wanted them to do.

Sometimes the prophets told people that God was angry, and they must change the way they lived. All the prophets felt that God was telling them what they had to say.

The Jewish family

Jews are one of the oldest groups of people in the world. There have been Jews for over 4,000 years.

But being Jewish is not just a religion, it is a way of living. It is important to most Jews. They feel that to be Jewish is like belonging to a huge family. They care what happens to other Jews, even people they have never met.

Some Jews today may not pay much attention to the religion in their daily life. But they often still feel that they share things in common with Jews around the world. No Jew today can really trace their family back to the time of Moses or the prophets, but most Jews still feel that the people who lived then matter to Jews today. This means that the history of the Jews is very important to them, because they feel that they are part of the same people.

Abraham

This section tells you about a man called Abraham.

Abraham lived about 4,000 years ago in a beautiful city called Ur. This was in the country that today we call Iraq. Abraham was rich and important. He had a good life, but he was not happy. He saw people in Ur **worshipping** gods of the sun and moon. He felt that this was wrong. He became sure that there was another God who was more important.

Abraham's journey

Abraham felt that this God was telling him to leave Ur.

He set out on a long journey. He took his wife Sarah, his servants, and all his animals. People who wander from place to place are called **nomads**. They do not have a fixed home. Usually nomads travel from one place to another to find water for their animals.

Abraham's journey was different – he and his family did not know where they were going, but Abraham believed God was leading him. Jews believe that God showed Abraham the way to the country called Canaan, which was more or less the country we now call Israel.

Moon gods in Ur were worshipped in special temples like this, called ziggurats.

These nomads still live in much the same way as Abraham did.

Jews believe that God made a promise to Abraham. He promised to look after Abraham's children for ever.

God's promise to Abraham

The Book of Genesis is part of the **Torah**. In the Book of Genesis, this is how God promises to give the land of Canaan to Abraham and his descendants. (Descendants means children and their children.)

God said, "Look carefully in all directions. I am going to give you and your descendants all the land that you see, and it will be yours for ever. I am going to give you so many descendants that no one will be able to count them – it would be as easy to count all the specks of dust on the earth! Now, go and look over all the land, because I am going to give it all to you."

(Genesis, chapter 13 verses 14–17)

Moses

This section tells you about a man called Moses.

When Moses was alive, the Jews were living in Egypt. The king of Egypt was afraid of the Jews, because he thought that they might try to take over his country. He ordered that all Jewish baby boys should be killed as soon as they were born. This was so that they could not grow up to fight against him.

Moses is rescued

When Moses was born, he too should have been killed. But his mother made a plan to save her son. She hid the baby in a basket by the side of the river.

The king's daughter came to the river to wash. She found the baby, and took him back to the palace. He lived as if he was the princess's own son.

When Moses grew up, he became the Jews' leader. He rescued them from Egypt. (This is the story which Jews remember at Pesach.) He was their leader while they spent many years as **nomads** living in the desert. At last, they found their way to the country of Canaan, which we call Israel.

Jews believe that while they were in the desert, God gave Moses the **Torah**.

This Egyptian painting shows the Jews working for the king.

The Covenant

The Torah tells Jews how to live. Jews believe that the Torah is part of a special agreement, called the **Covenant**. It is like a sort of bargain, where both sides make a promise. Jews believe God promised to take special care of them. In return, Jews promised they would keep the rules which God gave.

The life of Moses

The Chosen People

Jews are often called the Chosen People. In the Torah, God says "I have chosen you out of all people on the earth". Some people who are not Jews have not understood this. They think it means that God chose the Jews to be his favourites. It does not mean this. It is part of the Covenant which God made with the Jews.

The Covenant was an agreement made between God and the Jews. God promised to look after the Jews, but in return they must obey the laws which God gave. Jews believe that everybody should love and worship God, but only Jews have to obey the 613 rules in the Torah (see page 14). This means that being the Chosen People makes the Jews' life harder, not easier. They have extra responsibilities.

Persecution

This section tells you about the persecution of the Jews.

Persecution means being punished for what you believe. Ever since Judaism began, Jews have been persecuted because of their beliefs. No one really knows why. One reason is probably because keeping their religion and their own way of doing things has always been important for Jews. Some people have not understood what Jews believe. Often people are afraid of people or beliefs they do not understand.

Jews in Nazi Germany had to wear a yellow Star of David badge.

Persecution by the Nazis

The worst persecution of the Jews happened when the **Nazis** ruled Germany in the 1930s and 1940s. Their leader, Adolf Hitler, believed that people with blond hair and blue eyes were better than everyone else. He began to persecute many other groups.

Not liking somebody because of their religion or the colour of their skin is called **prejudice**. Hitler was prejudiced against the Jews. He made laws which said Jews could not do things like own shops or cars, or go to school. The list went on and on.

Then the Nazis decided to get rid of Jews completely. Soldiers went from one house to the next, asking if there were any Jews there. Any Jews they found were taken away. Anyone found hiding Jews was killed.

This sculpture is a part of the memorial at Yad Vashem to Jews killed by the Nazis

The Jews who were taken away were taken to special camps. They were treated very badly in these camps. They were not given enough food or clothes, and all their hair was shaved off. Many were killed straight away. Others died from illness or from lack of food.

By the end of the World War II in 1945, six million Jews had died. This was one Jew out of every three Jews alive in the world. Six million is a number too big to imagine: it is like one in ten of all the people in Britain today, or every person in London.

Anne Frank

Anne Frank was a Jewish girl whose family had moved to Holland from Germany to escape the Nazis. When the Nazis took over Holland, the family lived in secret rooms behind offices owned by Anne's father. For two years, they hid there. The people who had worked for her father brought them food, risking punishment and death.

Anne wrote a diary which tells about their life. Then, someone told the Nazis about the hiding place. The family were found and taken to a camp. Anne's mother, her sister, and then Anne herself, died. Her father was taken to a different camp, and he lived. After the war, Anne's father published her diary and we can still read it today.

Modern Jewish history

This section tells you about Jewish history in the last 60 years.

Israel

Millions of Jews were killed in World War II. When the war ended, many people thought Jews should have a country where they could be safe. At that time Jews lived all over the world. There was no "Jewish country". Israel was made a separate country in 1948. Every Jew in the world has the right to go and live in Israel if they want to. There is a picture of the flag of Israel on page 9.

Making Israel a separate country caused problems, because people were living there already. They are called Arabs.

Many Jews make a journey to the Western Wall in Jerusalem to pray.

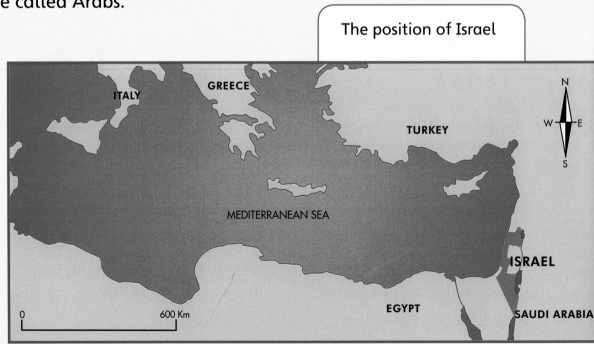

The position of Israel

ITALY
GREECE
TURKEY
MEDITERRANEAN SEA
ISRAEL
EGYPT
SAUDI ARABIA

N
W E
S

0　　　　600 Km

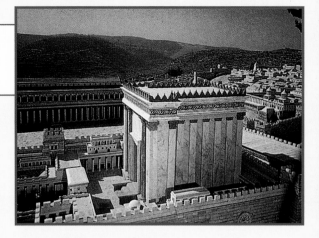

This model shows what the Temple in Jerusalem looked like.

The Arabs thought that the whole country should belong to them. Their families had lived there for hundreds of years. The problems were greater because parts of the country were important to **Christians** and **Muslims** too.

Wars between Jews and Arabs

After Israel became a separate country, there were wars between Israel and the countries around it. The Jews said that Israel was their land. The Arabs said it was theirs. This is why there is still fighting in that part of the world today. Many people have tried to sort out the problems, but it is difficult to get all the countries to agree.

The Temple

The **Temple** was the most important place of **worship** for Jews. The first Temple was built in Jerusalem by King Solomon almost 3,000 years ago. It was destroyed when the Jews' country was taken over by soldiers from the country of Babylon, in 586 BCE. Then it was built again, but it was destroyed by the Roman army in 70 CE.

The Temple was a beautiful building, decorated with gold and marble. Jews believe it was the **holiest** place in the world, and it was the most important place for worshipping God. Only one wall was left when it was destroyed. It is called the Western Wall. This is the reason why the Western Wall is so important – it is all that is left of the most important building the Jews have ever had.

Judaism now

This section tells you about different Jewish groups.

Not all members of a religion have exactly the same beliefs. Different groups of Jews do not all have exactly the same ideas. They all believe in the most important teachings, but they live their lives in different ways.

The largest group of Jews in the world today are called Orthodox Jews. About three Jews in every four living in Britain are Orthodox Jews.

Other Jews make up smaller groups, for example Liberal Jews and Reformed Jews, but they can all be called **Progressive Jews**.

Orthodox Jews

Orthodox Jews are often called "strict" Jews. They try to keep all the laws of Judaism as they have been kept for thousands of years.

Inside a Progressive synagogue

They believe that the **Torah** is the word of God. It tells people how God wants them to live, and people should follow the rules it gives. The Torah will never change, although its teaching may not always be seen in the same way. They feel that through the Torah, people can always know what God wants.

Progressive Jews

Progressive Jews are not all the same, but they all believe that Judaism can change. They do not keep all the laws of the Torah as strictly as Orthodox Jews. They study the laws and then, taking guidance from the **rabbi**, may decide that some laws are not important for Jews today. The changes in the laws usually make it easier to live among people who are not Jews.

Orthodox Jews studying the Scriptures

Differences between Orthodox and Progressive synagogues

Orthodox
- Men sit separately from women
- Men wear special clothes for **worship**
- Men always lead the worship
- Musical instruments are not usually used
- Services are always held using the Jewish language, **Hebrew**

Progressive
- Men and women sit together
- Special clothes are not usually worn
- Worship is led by men and women
- Musical instruments are often used
- Services are often held in the people's own language

Jewish belief at home

This section tells you a little about how Jews follow their religion at home.

Being a Jew is not just about going to the **synagogue**. It is about the way you live, too. Being Jewish affects every part of a Jew's life.

Mezuzot

A **mezuzah** is a tiny **scroll**. It has the prayer called the **Shema** written on it. The scroll has a cover over it to protect it.

The cover with the scroll inside it is fastened next to a door, always on the right hand side of the doorpost. Some Jews have a mezuzah next to the doors which lead in and out of the house. Other Jews have them fixed to the side of every door in the house, except those of the bathroom and toilet. As they pass the mezuzah, Jews touch it. This helps to remind them that God is always there.

This man is writing a mezuzah scroll.

A mezuzah fixed by a front door

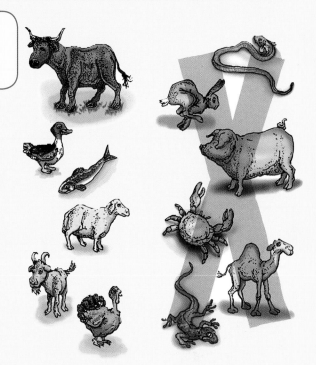

The foods on the left are kosher, those on the right are not.

Food

The **Torah** has many laws about food. There are laws about what foods can or cannot be eaten, and how food should be prepared. Many Jews keep these laws very carefully.

Food which Jews may eat is called **kosher**. Jews do not eat some meat at all. They do not eat dairy foods (such as butter and milk) at the same time as meat. They usually wait about three hours before "mixing" them.

As well as this, plates, cutlery, and cooking pots for meat and dairy foods should be kept separate. Because of this, some Jews have two sets, and two sinks or washing-up bowls.

Kosher foods

The laws about what foods Jews can and cannot eat are in the Torah.

All plants are kosher, but must be checked to make sure they do not contain any pests or insects, which would make them not kosher. Animals which chew the cud and have hooves divided in two are kosher. So Jews can eat meat from cows, sheep, goats, or deer, but they cannot eat meat from pigs, rabbits, or camels. Fish are kosher if they have fins and scales, but shellfish are not. Many birds are not kosher, and Jews do not normally eat any birds except chickens, turkeys, and ducks.

Keeping these rules is important for many Jews, because they believe that obeying God's law is part of **worship**.

Special occasions in childhood

This section tells you about Bar Mitzvah and Bat Mitzvah services.

Bar Mitzvah

On the **Shabbat** after a Jewish boy's 13th birthday, he takes part in the **synagogue service** for the first time. He says the prayer before the **Torah** is read in the service. Like all the prayers in an Orthodox service, this is in **Hebrew**. Some boys read the Torah, too.

Often, friends and relatives of the boy come to the service, and there may be a special meal afterwards.

Bar Mitzvah means "Son of the Commandments". Once he is this age, a Jewish boy is counted as a man. He can be one of the 10 men who must be present before a full service can be held in an Orthodox synagogue.

After his Bar Mitzvah, a Jewish boy is expected to obey all of the Jewish laws.

A Bar Mitzvah ceremony in a synagogue in Jerusalem

This Bat Mitzvah girl is holding a copy of the **holy** books which she has decorated.

Bat Mitzvah

A Jewish girl becomes Bat Mitzvah at the age of 12. Bat Mitzvah means "Daughter of the Commandments". In Progressive synagogues, there is no difference between the services held for boys and girls.

Not all Orthodox synagogues have a special service for girls. If there is one, it is held on a Sunday rather than on Shabbat (which is a Saturday). Girls do not read from the Torah in an Orthodox synagogue.

My Bar Mitzvah

"I was quite nervous when the day came for my Bar Mitzvah. I'd worked hard to learn the Hebrew, and I thought I'd be OK. But no matter how much I'd prepared it, it's different when you have to read in front of all the people in the synagogue. It was even harder because all my family and lots of friends were there, too.

When we got to the part of the service where the Torah **scroll** was brought out of the **Ark**, I knew I was shaking, and I was sure everyone could hear my heart thumping! But once I started reading, it was OK. In the end, I was almost sorry when it was over. Now, I feel really proud that I can be counted as a man."

David, aged 13

Marriage and death

This section tells you about what happens at Jewish marriage services and funerals.

Marriage

A Jewish wedding usually takes place in a **synagogue**. It is led by a **rabbi**. The couple who are getting married stand under a special covering. It is called a **huppah**. The huppah is a sign of the home they will share.

The huppah is beautifully decorated with flowers.

The couple drink from a glass of wine which has had prayers said over it. Then the marriage promises are read out, in which the bridegroom promises to look after his wife. The bride and groom sign them. The bridegroom gives the bride a ring, which she wears on the first finger of her right hand.

The bride and groom stand under the huppah.

At the end of the service, the bridegroom steps on a wine glass and breaks it. (It is wrapped in a cloth so it does not do any damage.) No one really knows why this happens, but it has been part of the marriage service for hundreds of years. It reminds the couple that there will be difficult things as well as good things in their life together.

Death

Jews believe that a funeral service should be held as soon as possible after someone dies. It is usually held within 24 hours. Services are simple, because Jews believe that there should be no differences for rich people or poor people. Everyone has to die. Most Jews do not agree with cremation – burning a body after death – because they think it destroys what God has made.

Jewish graves

Funeral customs

A Jewish writing says that when a man leaves the world, silver and gold will not go with him, nor any precious stones. The only thing that he can take with him is the **Torah** he has learned and the good things that he has done in his life.

   If it is possible for the person who is dying to speak, they will repeat the **Shema**, which sums up their belief in God. Jews believe that it is not right for a person to be alone when they die, and if possible their family will be with them. After the person has died, the body will never be left alone until it is buried. Jews do not believe that death is the end, but teaching about life after death is not very important in Judaism.

FALKIRK COUNCIL
LIBRARY SUPPORT
FOR SCHOOLS

Glossary

Adonai Jewish name for God

Ark cupboard where the scrolls are kept

bimah raised part of the synagogue where the reading desk is

challah bread bread specially baked for Shabbat and festivals

Christian follower of the religion of Christianity

commandment important rule

Covenant special agreement made between God and the Jews

fast go without food and drink for religious reasons

Feast of Weeks another name for Shavuot

greggor rattle used at Purim to drown out the name of Haman

hanukiah candle with eight branches used when celebrating Hanukkah

Hanukkah eight-day Jewish festival of lights

havdalah ceremony that ends Shabbat

Hebrew the Jewish language

holy to do with God

huppah covering used in marriage service

kippah small cap worn by Jewish males

kosher food which Jews can eat

leaven yeast or baking powder, which makes dough rise

matzot flat "crackers" of bread made without leaven (one is called a matzah)

menorah candlestick with seven branches

mezuzah tiny scroll containing a section from the Torah, often placed on doorposts of Jewish homes

Muslim follower of the religion of Islam

Nazis people who ruled Germany in the 1930s and 1940s

nomad a person who does not have a fixed home

Patriarchs the very first Jewish leaders

persecution being badly treated because of your religion

plague disaster or terrible event sent by God

prejudice to dislike someone because of their religion or colour

Progressive Jews members of Reform and Liberal groups

prophet a man or woman who tells people what God wants

psalm special poem used in worship

rabbi Jewish teacher

scroll rolled-up "book" on which the Torah is written

Seder special Pesach meal

service special meeting for worship

Shabbat Jewish day of rest and worship

Shema important Jewish prayer

shofar musical instrument made from a ram's horn (for more than one, you say shofarot)

spirit a being who is alive but does not have a body

sukkah sort of hut (for more than one you say sukkot)

synagogue Jewish place of worship

tallit prayer shawl

tefillin small leather boxes which contain writing from the Torah (one box is called a tefillah)

Temple most important place of worship for Jews

Ten Commandments rules for living which God gave to Moses

Torah Books of Teaching, part of the Jewish holy books

worship to show respect and love for God

Writings name given to the third part of the Jewish holy books

Find out more

More books to read

Barnes, Trevor. *World Faiths: Judaism*, Kingfisher, 2005.

Keene, Michael. *21st Century religions: Judaism*. London, Hodder Wayland, 2005.

Penney, Sue. *World beliefs and cultures: Judaism*. Oxford, Heinemann Library, 2001

Using the internet

You can find out more about Judaism in books and on the Internet. Use a search engine such as **www.yahooligans.com** to search for information. A search for the word "Judaism" will bring back lots of results, but it may be difficult to find the information you want. Try refining your search to look for some of the people and ideas mentioned in this book, such as "story of Abraham" or "Hanukkah".

Website

www.bbc.co.uk/religion/religions/judaism/index
Try looking here for up-to-date information and articles on Judaism and Jews.

Index